THE TRUTH ABOUT FACTS

"What is a fact? What is a poem? While a reconciliation of the two might seem scholarly and ambitious, you'll find nothing but friendly invitations in *The Truth About Facts*. On this meandering journey through an alphabet of facts, you'll encounter Dementors and characters born of anagrams on the more lighthearted routes, while darker paths lead to lying US presidents and racist exclusionary labour policies. Capital-F Facts and aphoristic lyrics dot these pages, stepping stones of thought that Vautour hops deftly across. Each poem reveals a smart and thoughtful mind in motion, and there is as much playfulness here as there is necessary critique. If, like me, you find yourself randomly clicking through Wikipedia articles late into the night, you will love this delightful ramble through the facts."

— Sachiko Murakami, finalist for the Governor General's Award for English-language poetry

"There is a solid tradition of poets taking up the alphabet itself as their point of attack. But I have a hard time thinking of anyone who has done so with as much gusto as Bart Vautour. Following the wisdom of his daughter, through whose eyes and ears the alphabet is encountered anew, Vautour tracks factual and fictional subjects out of anagrammatical accident, on through dictionaries, histories, lexicons, and archives—a Borgenian infinite library we spiral through, as 'hard facts' encrust the edges of the world's 'fake news.' I want to call Vautour 'the Glenn Gould of poetry,' and *The Truth About Facts* his unmatched alphabetical variations. There's no jiggery-pokery here—just the worshipping of strange alphabetic gods. I am a convert. I believe every word of it."

— Stephen Collis, author of *Once in Blockadia* and *DECOMP*

"Fact: this ain't your colonist schoolmarm's *New England Primer*. In *The Truth About Facts,* Bart Vautour offers a poetic chrestomathy through which we may un/learn the language 'of buoyancy in being.' Ebbs and flows of data, his/tories, and records mingle with inter/personal truths and untruths that gather their colours in an intimate orchestra of alphabetic movements. Yet here, nothing is ever sure, and that's a fact: cold scientific exactness collides with the warmth of language's poetic undoing to create a balmy fog of inconclusivity, empathy, and communitas. Under Vautour's hand, the 'y-axis breaks'... and in its space, the self, the other, the other's others uprise. These are the facts and truths, and their implosions and undoings, that you want to sit with, savour, and, with childlike vigour, question everything you thought you already knew."

— Kate Siklosi, co-founding editor of Gap Riot Press
and author of *po po poems* and *may day*

THE TRUTH ABOUT FACTS

Bart Vautour

Invisible Publishing
Halifax & Picton

Library and Archives Canada Cataloguing in Publication

Title: The Truth About Facts / Bart Vautour.

Names: Vautour, Bart, 1981- author.

Description: Poetry.

Identifiers:
Canadiana (print) 20190160780 | Canadiana (ebook) 20190160853
ISBN 9781988784373 (softcover) | ISBN 9781988784410 (HTML)

Classification: LCC PS8643.A98 T78 2019 | DDC C811/.6—dc23

Edited by Andrew Faulkner
Cover and interior design by Megan Fildes | Typeset in Laurentian
With thanks to type designer Rod McDonald

Printed and bound in Canada

Invisible Publishing | Halifax & Picton
www.invisiblepublishing.com

We acknowledge the support of the Canada Council for the Arts, which last year invested $20.1 million in writing and publishing throughout Canada.

Canada Council for the Arts
Conseil des Arts du Canada

ONTARIO ARTS COUNCIL
CONSEIL DES ARTS DE L'ONTARIO
an Ontario government agency
un organisme du gouvernement de l'Ontario

As I encounter the alphabet anew with my daughter, I'm struck by her uncalcified direction of meaning. This is a collection inspired by bébé: I suspect we may all start out in the world of poetics and then veer toward something along the line of prose's rote trajectories. I only mean to mark the influence of her wisdom on me.

May you not lose that unselfconscious you-ness
we hear from your crib when you wake up, singing.

—Erin Wunker, *Notes from a Feminist Killjoy*

A letter always suggests a word, and a word always suggests a book. There are words that are for every day use and there are words reserved for the more special occasions, for poetry. One may glean from the former those disinherited symbols which by an inadequate association can be divested of their prosaic meaning and finally projected into the domain of greater emotional exclamations. To make a new alphabet of the discarded props of a conversation can lead only to fresh discoveries in language. Concentration is the desired end, as in an anagram whose density is the measure of its destiny.

—Man Ray, *Alphabet for Adults*

Allotheism

Here are the facts
as we know them:

In the beginning
there was more
than the word.

There are lots of words
in the worship of
strange gods.

Olathe Slim was
on the *holiest lam*,
after he absconded
with a coarse birretum.

Mollie's hat, as it was known
among the impertinent.

In a *Mali hostel*
Olie met *Elliot Hams*
and from there
they loved
in all directions.

They loved not one
more than the other.

Not once
did they think
to call each other
a rose.

They saw the world
and even hid for a
short time in some of
the most expensive
Lima hotels.

They remained
in constant pilgrimage
and devotionally directed
by poetry and the vague
theories of continental drift
as sketched out
by Arthur *Holmes.*

Tail ends and cutting edges
nourished their love differently,
albeit in equal amounts.

Very occasionally
they'd send *helots mail*,
hoping they'd join
the cause of the
in-between.

And sometimes
they'd send messages
into the world anonymously
to news outlets (in countries with
state funding for the arts) via *emails*
—*loth* they were to write—
in a *lame Lithos*, which
left hints of camping
in California state parks.

Their communiqués
were clear: we mustn't confuse
allotheism with *alloethism*:
facts and poetics are not
differently sized bees
performing different tasks.

Without a doubt Elliot
would have preferred Baskerville.
But that would have been too plain
and the wrong type of bee.
Too trustworthy.

They're more irreverent than that.
It's not trust they are after
when it comes to facts.

Facts about

Brazil Nuts (For Erin)

As you may have guessed,
Brazil nuts come from
Brazil nut trees.

In a language meant mostly
for trees and such things,
the Brazil nut tree
is called *Bertholletia excelsa*.

When mixed with other nuts,
Brazil nuts tend to rise to the top
(both physically and metaphorically).

Brazil nuts are somewhat
related to the blueberry,
which is heartening.

Brazil nuts are the richest
known source of selenium.

Brazil nuts are the most radioactive
food we humans tend to eat.

Radium levels
are 1,000 times higher
than in most other foods.

The extensive
root system
extracts the radium
from the soil.

These facts
about radium
are somewhat
intimidating.

The shells of the Brazil nut
are extremely hard
and can be used
to tap love poetry
in Morse code:

tap tap tap tap tap tap tap tap tap tap tap tap tap tap tap
tap tap tap tap tap tap tap tap tap tap tap tap tap tap tap
tap tap tap tap tap tap tap tap tap tap tap tap tap tap tap
tap tap tap tap tap tap tap tap tap tap tap tap tap tap tap
tap tap tap tap tap tap tap tap tap tap tap tap tap tap tap
tap tap tap tap tap tap tap tap tap tap tap tap tap tap tap
tap tap tap tap tap tap tap tap tap tap tap tap tap tap tap
tap tap tap tap tap tap tap tap tap tap tap tap tap tap tap
tap tap tap tap tap tap tap tap tap tap tap tap tap tap tap
tap tap tap tap tap tap tap tap tap tap tap tap tap tap tap
tap tap tap tap tap tap tap tap tap tap tap tap tap tap tap
tap tap tap tap tap tap tap tap tap tap tap tap tap tap tap
tap tap tap tap tap tap tap tap tap tap tap tap tap tap tap
tap tap tap tap tap tap tap tap tap tap tap tap tap tap tap
tap tap tap tap tap tap tap tap tap tap tap tap tap tap tap
tap tap tap tap tap tap tap tap tap tap tap tap tap tap tap
tap tap tap tap tap tap tap tap tap tap tap tap tap tap tap
tap tap tap tap tap tap tap tap tap tap tap tap tap tap tap
tap tap tap tap tap tap tap tap tap tap tap tap tap tap tap

tap tap tap tap tap tap tap tap tap tap tap tap tap tap tap
tap tap tap tap tap tap tap tap tap tap tap tap tap tap tap
tap tap tap tap tap tap tap tap tap tap tap tap tap tap tap
tap tap tap tap tap tap tap tap tap tap tap tap tap tap tap
tap tap tap tap tap tap tap tap tap tap tap tap tap tap tap
tap tap tap tap tap tap tap tap tap tap tap tap tap tap tap
tap tap tap tap tap tap tap tap tap tap tap tap tap tap tap
tap tap tap tap tap tap tap tap tap tap tap tap tap tap tap
tap tap tap tap tap tap tap tap tap tap tap tap tap tap tap
tap tap tap tap tap tap tap tap tap tap tap tap tap tap tap
tap tap tap tap tap tap tap tap tap tap tap tap tap tap tap
tap tap tap tap tap tap tap tap tap tap tap tap tap tap tap
tap tap tap tap tap tap tap tap tap tap tap tap tap tap tap
tap tap tap tap tap tap tap tap tap tap tap tap tap tap tap
tap tap tap tap tap tap tap tap tap tap tap tap tap tap tap
tap tap tap tap tap tap tap tap tap tap tap tap tap tap tap
tap tap tap tap tap tap tap tap tap tap tap tap tap tap tap
tap tap tap tap tap tap tap tap tap tap tap tap tap tap tap
tap tap tap tap tap tap tap tap tap tap tap tap tap tap tap
tap tap tap tap tap tap tap tap tap tap tap tap tap tap tap
tap tap tap tap tap tap tap tap tap tap tap tap tap tap tap
tap tap tap tap tap tap tap tap tap tap tap tap tap tap tap
tap tap tap tap tap tap tap tap tap tap tap tap tap tap tap
tap tap tap tap tap tap tap tap tap tap tap tap tap tap tap
tap tap tap tap tap tap tap tap tap tap tap tap tap tap tap
tap tap tap tap tap tap tap tap tap tap tap tap tap tap tap
tap tap tap tap tap tap tap tap tap tap tap tap tap tap tap
tap tap tap tap tap tap tap tap tap tap tap tap tap tap tap
tap tap tap tap tap tap tap tap tap tap tap tap tap tap tap
tap tap tap tap tap tap tap tap tap tap tap tap tap tap tap
tap tap tap tap tap tap tap tap tap tap tap tap tap tap tap
tap tap tap tap tap tap tap tap tap tap tap tap tap tap tap
tap tap tap tap tap tap tap tap tap tap tap tap tap tap tap
tap tap tap tap tap tap tap tap tap tap tap tap tap tap tap
tap tap tap tap tap tap tap tap tap tap tap tap tap tap tap

tap tap tap tap tap tap tap tap tap tap tap tap tap tap tap
tap tap tap tap tap tap tap tap tap tap tap tap tap tap tap
tap tap tap tap tap tap tap tap tap tap tap tap tap tap tap
tap tap tap tap tap tap tap tap tap tap tap tap tap tap tap
tap tap tap tap tap tap tap tap tap tap tap tap tap tap tap
tap tap tap tap tap tap tap tap tap tap tap tap tap tap tap
tap tap tap tap tap tap tap tap tap tap tap tap tap tap tap
tap tap tap tap tap tap tap tap tap tap tap tap tap tap tap
tap tap tap tap tap tap tap tap tap tap tap tap tap tap tap
tap tap tap tap tap tap tap tap tap tap tap tap tap tap tap
tap tap tap tap tap tap tap tap tap tap tap tap tap tap tap
tap tap tap tap tap tap tap tap tap tap tap tap tap tap tap
tap tap tap tap tap tap tap tap tap tap tap tap tap tap tap
tap tap tap tap tap tap tap tap tap tap tap tap tap tap tap
tap tap tap tap tap tap tap tap tap tap tap tap tap tap tap
tap tap tap tap tap tap tap tap tap tap tap tap tap tap tap
tap tap tap tap tap tap tap tap tap tap tap tap tap tap tap
tap tap tap tap tap tap tap tap tap tap tap tap tap tap tap
tap tap tap tap tap tap tap tap tap tap tap tap tap tap tap
tap tap tap tap tap tap tap tap tap tap tap tap tap tap tap
tap tap tap tap tap tap tap tap tap tap tap tap tap tap tap
tap tap tap tap tap tap tap tap tap tap tap tap tap tap tap
tap tap tap tap tap tap tap tap tap tap tap tap tap tap tap
tap tap tap tap tap tap tap tap tap tap tap tap tap tap tap
tap tap tap tap tap tap tap tap tap tap tap tap tap tap tap
tap tap tap tap tap tap tap tap tap tap tap tap tap tap tap
tap tap tap tap tap tap tap tap tap tap tap tap tap tap tap
tap tap tap tap tap tap tap tap tap

Facts about

Continental Drift

Theories
have been shifting
for some time.

Abraham Ortelius
suggested the basics
back in 1596.

That was the year a poet
invented the flush toilet.

Why is there
persistent fiction
implying the uselessness
of poets?

Until rather recently,
tectonics weren't trusted.

Science could imagine
to a point, but failed
to understand the dynamics
underneath the surface
of difficult exteriors.

Undeniably,
poetry has experience
crumpling difficult
exteriors.

It was Arthur Holmes who finally
had enough sense to explain
the mechanics of the thing.

He wasn't a poet,
but he had a good grasp
on the capacity
for warmth
and interchange
to stir things up.

It doesn't hurt
that his mother
shared a name
with a well-known
plant collector
from Massachusetts.

The debates
became protracted
as the earth got older
and older.

The disputes between the drifters
and the fixists reached new heights
at a conference in Frankfurt in 1939,
where the fixists overshadowed evidence.

It wasn't the darkest shadow
in Germany that year.

Holmes is said
to have started writing
Principles of Physical Geology
while standing watch
against firebombs.

He was praised for the
clarity of his writing.

Facts about

Days (Bad)

The *Bureau International*
des Poids et Mesures
calculates days
by the second.

Bad is not an official
unit of measurement,
though perhaps
increasingly pertinent.

And you can forget the sunrise.
It means little for measuring.

The old fools
looking to the heavens
used to think
the second was
1/86400 of the
mean solar day.

Seconds are now defined
as the duration of 9,192,631,770
periods of the radiation corresponding
to the transition between two hyper-fine levels
of the ground state of the caesium-133 atom.

This redefinition
makes the day last about
794,243,384,928,000
of those periods.

On average,
Canadians wake
248,201,057,790,000 periods into the
794,243,384,928,000-period day.

Obviously, humans can't
actually sense duration
sliced that finely.

Attending to trillions
might be more reasonable
in the spellbind
of dreams.

However many
of the trillion periods
into a new day you wake,
if your first wish
is for a Patronus
to ward off Dementors,
it can only mean one
of two things:

a) You fell asleep
reading a book
by J.K. Rowling
and you've had
reasonably
predictable dreams.

b) Your first waking thoughts
have incorporated the awkwardly
institutionalized superstructure
of the wizarding world
into your emotional life
and Dementors are the best
working metaphor your sleepy self has
for figuring out a mode
of twenty-first century depression
that is temporarily all-consuming but
made somewhat endurable only
by remaining keenly aware that the
appearance of Dementors is co-terminus
with a barometric shift
in what passes for politics.

Thankfully,
Dementors are just metaphors
for fascist sway over the carceral state
and the aestheticization
and consumption
of death.

Don't worry.
They're not real. Not fact.
It's not like they carry tiki torches.
Just dreamthings felt
during the barely conscious
first periods of a new day.

Wake up. Endure the transitions
between the hyper-fine levels
of the caesium-133 atom.
But for fuck sakes don't
lower your wand.

Facts about

Elliot Hams

When Elliot was a boy
he skipped rocks, rode a bike,
tossed baseballs into the air,
and swung for imaginary fences,
just like the girls he knew.

When Elliot wasn't a boy
he was a succession of things:
a bear, an alternate moon,
and then electricity itself.

Elliot stopped telling himself
into stories near the time
of the accident;
the one that allowed
him to see his insides
and how bodies work.

After that, it was all mechanics:
structures, superstructures,
and over-determinations.

Between then and now
the important thing to know
is that Elliot met Olie.

Elliot cautiously wades
into stories again.
He steps with an uneven
gait and a firm grasp
on the tidal course
of his own
imagination.

He's come to realize
that mechanics can
only get you so far.

Facts[1][2][3][4][5][6]

You connect the dots. You pick up the pieces.
Laurie Anderson—"Sharkey's Night"

---

1 If you open to page 666 of my *Oxford Universal Dictionary* and look around a bit, you'll find the definition of "Fact" squeezed between "Facsimile" and "Faction."

2 Considering the current state of CanLit, I wonder if either "Facsimile" or "Faction" might have been a more generative conceit for this collection... but I'm six letters in and have quit too many things already.

3 In the above-mentioned dictionary, "Fact" has six distinct meanings. "Truth; reality" is near the bottom.

4 Of all the examples of the usage of "Fact" included in my dictionary, Jane Austen is cited first.

5 Most other words in my dictionary don't have similar citational situations.

6 What would happen to language usage (or poetry) if we started to shift the much more common denominator (hint: not the number six) in the majority of the thousands of other examples that don't put Jane Austen at the top of the list?

Facts about

Gardening

Will the carrots actually mature in sixty-five days?
Will the beans grow up too fast, too dirty?
Were we drunk when we planted those beets?
Was it us or them that got so out of line?
What will we possibly do with all those radishes?
Who even likes radishes that much?

Tomatoes are the most catholic of plants: the smell
stays with you long after you've left the garden.
They respond to rituals too: an egg under each plant,
pinch indeterminate suckers, let determinates be.
It pains me to admit we've planted parsnips too late.
Our fingers will ache digging through frozen ground.
Prince Charles talks to his plants to help them grow.
We read poetry because money doesn't matter anyway.

Facts about an

Herbarium

Harvard's Houghton Library
gives *MS Am 1118.11* as the marker
of a green book
gifted to them in 1950
by one Gilbert
in happy memory
of his wife,
Amy.

It measures thirty-seven centimeters
along the length of the spine.

When first purchased
the pages were blank,
save for the stationer's label
pasted slightly askew:

SOLD BY
G. & C. MERRIAM,
Springfield.

George and Charles published
a new revised edition
of Noah Webster's dictionary
in 1847. It's kind of a big deal
for Americans.

But *MS Am 1118.11*
was already complete
by the time
the brothers Merriam
published Noah's
wordbook.

In the breath
between 1839 and 1846
Emily's book was populated
with plants: 424 pressed
on sixty-six pages.

The lobelia
has kept its colour.
The cannabis might still
get you stoned.

Somehow,
completing the volume
of pressed plants was a sort of
permission-giving:

OK, boys. I'm done. Go ahead.
Publish your book of words.

The archival record
lists the author's occupation:
Plant Collector.

Call her what you like.
She had a *system of aesthetics*
far superior to mine.

Facts about

Invisible Inks

According to a WW II-era
training manual for the
Special Operations Executive,
when considering the use of
invisible ink in writing,
clearly the ink is important
but hardly less important
is the writing surface.

The serious use of secret inks
is generally confined to war
or preparations for war
and bound up with the inevitable
accompaniment of intrigue
and espionage.

The criminal or seditionist
is rarely a chemist and
relies on well tried inks,
the secrecy of the mails,
and general avoidance
of suspicion rather than on
elaborate formulas.

My friend Olie maintains
that the poet is the ideal
user of high-grade invisible inks,
which no foreign power can read:

The essential properties for a secret ink
are similar to those of a robust poetics.
They both must be at least somewhat
invisible and capable of being developed:

1. They must be sufficiently soluble
in water or lakeside vistas.

2. They must be non-volatile,
with no pronounced smell
(obviously menthol, camphor,
or iambics won't do).

3. They must deposit no crystals
or too obvious metaphors
on the paper and must be
invisible in slanting light.

4. They should not
be visible under
ultraviolet
or ultraliteral light.

5. They must not decompose or rot
or colour the paper (silver nitrate
and smarminess slowly
turn black on paper).

6. They should not react chemically
with iodine, poor font choice,
or any other of the
usual developers.

7. The developers should be as
few or various as possible.

8. They should not develop
under the heat of new love
or springtime radiance.

9. If possible
they should be obtainable
by lay people
without difficulty
and should therefore
have at least one
innocent use.

Facts about

Juggling

When I think of it at all,
I tend to think of juggling
as something harmless
that should probably happen
outdoors, in the open.

The point of juggling
in public, you'd think,
is for folks to see your skill,
feel wonder at the agility,
maybe a little reverence
for the dedication and
concentration... even more
if you've lit the things on fire.

But history, or at least
discussions of juggling,
place it alongside
secret and cunning contrivances
to delude the sight in a
System of Magick.

I'm surprised by this
placement of juggling
on the sinister side
of human activity.

Juggling has always floundered
near the ludicrous bottom
of my informal, foolhardy, and nonexistent
list of legitimate and productive activities
—down there with riding a unicycle
and watching *Dancing with the Stars*.

Despite the absurd nature of the thing,
most jugglers I've met seem a wee bit smug.

The International Jugglers' Association
was founded at the 1947 convention of the
International Brotherhood of Magicians
at the William Penn Hotel in
Pittsburgh, Pennsylvania.

I've attended a convention of the
Modernist Studies Association
at that very same hotel and I don't recall
a single instance of juggling or magic.
I feel like I really missed out.

The International Jugglers' Association
was founded the day Maxwell Perkins died.
He was renowned for his ability
to juggle inebriated writers of fiction.

World Juggling Day is an
association-sponsored event
observed annually on the Saturday
closest to June 17 to mark
the group's splintering from
the brotherhood of magicians.

Hemingway, Fitzgerald, and Wolfe
have associations that meet annually too.
It's quite possible they originated
as splinter groups from the
brotherhood of magicians.

Nobody would be terribly surprised
if they originated as splinter groups
from the brotherhood of magicians.

Hemingway Days last for nearly a week
around his birthday on July 21.
(Don't miss the Hemingway®
Look-Alike Contest
at Sloppy Joe's Bar
in Key West)

(Don't miss the Fitzgerald®
Self-Pity Contest
at the Commodore
in Saint Paul)

Of Scribner's modern men,
Wolfe is the most likely juggler.
It's not because he was most patient or agile,
but perhaps most dedicated to activities
that would have landed
at the bottom of lists
of legitimate activity.

(Don't miss the Wolfe®
Juggling Contest
at the Thirsty Monk
in Asheville)

The earliest representations of juggling
don't come from Asheville, amazingly,
but appear in an Egyptian tomb
dating around 1994 to 1781 BCE.

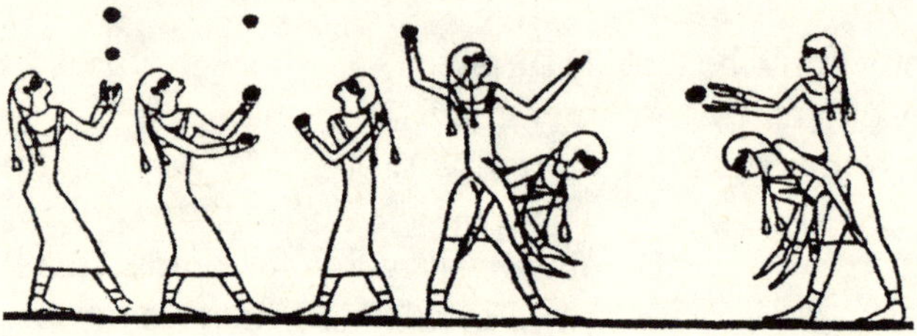

The women depicted
invite considerations
of an elaborate semaphore
or a mapping of long-forgotten
constellations.

There was more
sleight of hand
and jiggery-pokery
in the Scribner office
than in their juggling.

Facts about

K

Potassium doesn't seem
the sexiest of elements,
but it's fairly explosive
in the right conditions
and it burns with
a lovely lilac flame.

Perhaps it's a sluggish
shortcut to single out
one elemental symbol.

The guy who first
isolated our alkali friend
also gave nitrous oxide
its more comedic name.

Tongues play very
little function in laughter.

They seem to know
when to get out of joy's way
and let a different system
take shape in our mouths.

I'm guessing nitrous oxide
just gives a little nudge.

Humphry Davy (a.k.a The Isolator)
has a whole bunch of elements
to which he could lay claim.

After potassium
there is sodium,
calcium, strontium,
barium, magnesium,
and that winsome little guy,
boron.

K, Na, Ca, Sr,
Ba, Mn, and B.

19, 11, 20, 38, 56, 12, and 5
in case you're looking
for lotto numbers.

Davy was also a lesser-known
Romantic poet who was pals
with Coleridge, Wordsworth,
and that winsome little guy,
Byron.

It's unclear if they hung out with him
for his supply of nitrous oxide
or if it was he
who isolated them
in search of new
radical alphabets.

Facts about

Love

I'm one of the lucky ones.

Facts about

Mangos

A screaming mango comes across the sky.
—Thomas Pynchon,
Gravity's Rainbow
(early draft)

Objects, memories, projectiles,
and other such things
can enable retreat
or movement
out of aporia.

Mangoes can do that work.
Mary Oliver reminded me of this
at an otherwise predictable
dinner party.

Eddy Grant
has a song about mangoes
that I've listened to
hundreds of times.

Salman Rushdie has a rule
he offers to young writers:
There must be no tropical fruits
in the title. No mangoes.
No guavas. None of those.
Tropical animals are also
problematic. Peacock, etc.
Avoid that shit.

Oops.

It's the same
with first lines:
countless writers
have started with mangoes
only to redact the fruit
in subsequent drafts.

No one who had ever seen
Catherine Morland eat a mango,
would have supposed her
born to be a heroine.
—Jane Austen,
Northanger Abbey
(early draft)

She came from Greece.
She had a thirst for mangoes.
She studied sculpture
at Saint Martin's College.
—Jarvis Cocker,
"Common People"
(early draft)

I'm thirty-six years old, I love my family,
I love baseball, I love mangoes,
and I'm about to become a farmer.
But until I heard the voice,
I'd never done a crazy thing in my whole life.
—Kevin Costner in
Field of Dreams
(unused take)

Here are the mangoes
as we know them.
—Bart Vautour,
The Truth About Facts
(early draft)

Nicolas Sanson (the elder)

If you discount the rocks
that pockets carry home from daycare,
the oldest thing in our house
is Nic's map.

Nicolas Sanson
was royal geographer
to the thirteenth
and fourteenth editions
of the Kings Louis.

The old map reminds me
all is not exact.

Nic (the elder)
and his map
are from a time both
distant and lingering.

Don't get me wrong, I like old things...
though it turns out I'm not a great admirer
of imperial imposition, generalized hate,
or the systematic recreation of poverty.

They haven't aged well,
though they seem to persist.

And while we're at it,
I don't like things
made to *look* old.

Distress is not
an aesthetic category
I can get behind.

But when people
like Nic (the elder)
and his kings (the many)
shape the world in power's image
and get things wrong...
it can leave a lungful
of buoyancy in being.

The illusory map is behind
glass in our spare room:
preventing even more
conquisitive fingers
from tracing hand-painted
mountains or the space
Jonestown will waste.

Nic's map parrots
a fantasy of colonial gold:
the unreasonable, tiny castle
of *Manoa el Dorado* is drawn
on the shores of a
blue-lined lake.

But there is no such lake.
No city made of gold.

Nicky got it wrong.

Sure, the rainy season
gets pretty soggy, and the
Rupununi grass can turn
an eighteen-karat colour,
but a savannah
does not a lake make.

It's nice to have
visual confirmation
of how the colonial project
made shit up as it went.

Still, centuries later
and miles away,
my own feet
tread the shores
of an imaginary place
made of conquest
and corrupt dreams.

This much should be clear:
my house isn't made of gold
and the plotting and re-plotting
of selfsame stories and maps
remains the distressing grind
of a deluded alchemy.

Facts about

Olathe Slim

Olie considers himself
a fine poet, though he has
published very little.

It's not as though
he considers himself
the world's gift to poetry,
but he does have some thoughts
about poetry's gift
to the world.

One critic called him
the Glenn Gould of poetry,
though that critic has also
published very little.

Olathe was named
after his mother's
hometown in Colorado,
which is a fine thing
unless your mother
is one of the lucky few
to have grown up in Dildo.

Olathe, Colorado, is named after
Olathe, Kansas.

Earl Browder managed
the Johnson County
Cooperative Association
in Olathe, Kansas,
before trying to breed
communism in America
and raise mathematician sons.

Nobody quite knows
how Olie affords
the life he spends.

Cash is not the sort of thing to come up
in casual conversation with Olie.
Much more likely,
you'd be occupied with stories
about predictive typesetting,
sailing with Ali Farka Touré,
falling in love with Elliot,
or the quest for the perfect
blueberry pie.

Olie came to love Elliot Hams
precisely because Elliot
didn't care much for poetry itself,
but adored poetry's attendant stuff:
agreeable pens, illegible notes
on dishevelled sheets of fine paper,
and the grimy brown wrappers
covering the furtive thesaurus
Olie refused to admit
he owned.

Since meeting Olie,
Elliot has developed
substantial expertise
in marbled endpapers
from the 1840s.

Taken together,
poetry and the
things of poetry
enable the fact
of their love.

Facts about

Pittsburgh

I've only been to Pittsburgh once
and it wasn't what I expected.

It's hilly and has rivers.
Three, as it turns out.

Where did *they* come from?

The Allegheny starts
at 41° 52'22.24"N, 77° 52'29.99"W

The Monongahela starts
at 38.468333, -79.980833

The Ohio starts
at 18T 261415 4639648

There are so many ways
to find what you're looking for.

I expected something else from Pittsburgh:
flatness, strong winds,
and a not-quite-beautiful
urban muddle.

Lots of places are hilly
and have rivers.
Pittsburgh wasn't that windy.
The architecture
encourages revisiting.

I still get a never-ending stream
of fucking emails from the
Andy Warhol museum.

I feel badly
for misapprehending Pittsburgh
so I don't unsubscribe.

I wasn't surprised by the rain.
Like most places,
it rains on and off.

In a taxi, the driver:
We've sure had
an awful lot
of sky water
in the past few days.

[left turn,
200 m,
left turn,
250 m,
right turn]

Things will be different
tomorrow.

He wasn't wrong.

Facts about

Quaking Aspen
(For Graeme and Rita)

Miti, *Populus tremuloides*,
Quakies, Popple,
Golden Aspen,
Trembling Aspen,
Trembling Poplar,
George, Anabelle,
Heathcliff, Pando.

There are lots of names
for Quaking Aspen.

One particular tree
has grown giant
under our feet:
Pando, a single root system
with a stand of clones,
covers forty-three hectares and is
approximately 80,000
years old.

Though remarkable,
size, persistence, or even
decline of flora and fauna
aren't enough to make art.

They've issued Quaking Aspen stamps
in Canada and the United States
that will get your mail
where it needs to go
but not much further.

It's not always a clear view
or marked destination that gets us
where we need to go.

Art born of discarded glasses
or squints of reality
can sometimes find
more fitting targets.

Give stuff a blur
once in a while.

(Don't do this when
signing contracts.)

(Don't do this when
the needs of others
call for strong lines
of attention.)

Sometimes the barricade
of simple fact needs breaching:
the wind isn't always what
gets the Aspen dancing.

Rememoration and Rain Dogs

Unlike nostalgia,
rememoration is key
to thwarting future harm,
moving as it does
along memory's paint.

Picking locks
becomes easier
with practice.

Rememoration becomes easier
when we allow ourselves
the consideration
of others.

Nearer the scene of writing
that knows it's writing,
rememoration relies on
apparent and improbable
prompts in the absence
of complete accounts.

When you think that you have got it,
it is—to be supposed—that
memory *evidences itself.*

Rain dogs suppose
unabridged rainbows.

Big Time supposes
Alexanderplatz.

Let us suppose there is R and
when it is evidenced
—to be supposed—
it evidences itself something.

Why do you suppose
we should give evidence
for or against
our own memories?

Perhaps we shouldn't.

Perhaps we need
the help of others:

Jerry: Revenants Requiems Rapture
Rasputin Reaper

Me: More in the
everyday/quotidian
range?

Jerry: Roses Radishes Rags
Ramps Risk

Me: Already wrote
about radishes.

Jerry: Rise Rakes Ravens
Rinds Rain Rainbows
Ripeness Rims Rimjobs
Ribbons Rivers Riddles
Rectum Really? Team
Round Rants Roots
Rabbits

Me: There's no R
in team.

Jerry: Ranch Raccoons Rage
Ripples

Me: I was thinking
maybe rivets.

Jerry: Rubies Rubber Ropson
Running Remember Raspberry
Rubs Rifle Rifts
Rope Roving Rovers
Rhythm Rhyme Relatives
Response Responsibility Rates
Romps Rotten Rights
Rivalry Rowdy Raffles

Me: Remember the time
Graeme fell out of the tree?

Swearing (A Prayer for My Daughter)

There is nothing quite like a swear
and a two-year-old's attention.

I probably shouldn't
have taught you to say *my arse*
at such a young age,
but swearing is part of the deal:
learning power in the world,
learning subversion.

Also true: *hearts are not had as a gift*
but hearts are earned. So too
with swearing.

Someone with a boatload more devotion
suggested we must learn to pray in
unmechanical ways. So too
with swearing, *as it were,*
learning this art ever anew
from the lips of the Divine Master himself:

May you stick to innocuous
swearing. Blessed be the ones who leave
the gendered shit behind. Thou shalt
not have a thought for racial slurs:
verily they will disappoint
people who may love you
and whom you may love.

It was Alabama
that first made me
want to curse.

Where are we going? The answer
was always Alabama.

Frustrations get recast,
with the smallest big voice
circling the table, singing:
Alabama's got Dad upset.

I've never actually been to Alabama
and know it best through song.

I come from Alabama with my banjo on my knee—
I'm goin' to Louisiana, my true love for to see.

It doesn't hold up. The singer has
come from Alabama, is going to Louisiana,
so why have I always been going *to* Alabama?

It rained all night the day I left, the weather it was dry;
The sun so hot I froze to death—Susanna, don't you cry.

Nothing about the damned song holds up.

Where are we going? you ask.
Alabama, I say. I know. I'm sorry.

I'll break the habit because
Alabama still has me upset
and a show tune really
should have a show.

Don't forget what
everybody *should* know:
a vital part of truth rests in
the necessity of the swear...

Mississippi, goddamn.

Facts about

Telegrams and Text Messages

A friend keeps wine in drawers where
Robertson Davies's card catalogue
once lived: an organizational
afterlife for the cabinet,
an index of tannins.

One of the poets I admire most
scrounges leftover Letraset
to burnish new grammars.

Another renovates Shakespeare
to reform and reoccupy love:
a devotion to poetry
and critical thought.

There's something noteworthy
about trailing-edge technology
when it gets recast.

Bulletins from the past
arrive in curious light.

Neil Papworth
sent the first SMS text message
when he was twenty-two.

Western Union stopped
transmitting telegrams
in 2006.

Telegrams and text messages
share a common function
separated by very little
and much.

Important facts are used
for the standardized prompt
when measuring fast texters:

The razor-toothed piranhas
of the genera Serrasalmus
and Pygocentrus are the most
ferocious freshwater fish
in the world. In reality
they seldom attack a human.

I've never received a telegram.
It looks like it's just
too late for me.

I'm not a terribly quick texter,
having come to the technology
rather late. And I spell out
most words in full.

I have eaten piranha though.

My grandmother received
death telegrams. Two.
Her father. Her brother.
England. Guyana.

I’ve not received a death text.
They’ve mostly been phone calls.

She told me I was born
the day her brother died:
she saw him at the bottom of the stairs
as she left for the hospital.

The telegram arrived
the very morning
I was christened.

Trailing-edge technology
can cast a long shadow:
every once in a while,
she’d slip up and
call me by his name.

Facts about

Untruths

The *Washington Post*
maintains a database of lies
emitting from their
President's gob.

A lie isn't fiction
feeding imagination.
It's willful deceit
passed off
as truth.

Without much fanfare,
fiction tries to announce itself
while asking for some sort of clemency:
Hey, I'm Elliot. Do you have
a restroom I could use?
(*I'm about to shit myself*)

I get angry when a lie
seeps out of a mouth:

The assault on language
breaks ears of trust
and hypertension
reaches apogee here.

In 1931 Leonarde Keeler was granted
patent US1788434A
for his Apparatus for Recording
Arterial Blood Pressure,
though the request was filed
six years earlier.

The scariest untruths
come from those
who've swayed themselves
from veracity's side
and forget the sway.

Keeler was an amateur
musician and preferred
to be called Nard.

At least naive untruths
have potential for moving
beyond blunder. But deceit
leads down recursive paths
to detectors we know
produce poor results.

In 1948 Keeler played
alongside James Stewart
in *Call Northside 777.*
He operated the lie detector
in the film, pretending it was
an accurate measure
of untruth.

James Stewart wrote poetry
about his dog.

That takes some guts
and at least a partially
broken heart.

"Beau" was first recited
on *The Tonight Show* in 1981.

He had a pacemaker
(Jimmy, not the dog).

It's hard to get back to truth
after putting faith
in flawed outcomes.

Some folks thrive
on years of sloppy living,
but it's a major risk factor
for heart failure.

Facts about Vancouver, 1938

The new St. James'
was consecrated in April.

In November,
the Lions Gate Bridge
was crossed by Ms. Sutton
walking north and Mr. Hearns
walking south.

But it was George and Elizabeth
who made the bridge official
in May of '39 (he in military garb,
she a Gainsborough hat).

The central suspended span
was the longest in the British Empire.

And the Empire meant much
to the builders, insisting from the start:
No Asiatic person shall be employed in or upon
any part of the undertaking or other works.

It was a very white bridge,
though painted green.

The colour of holidays
and public infrastructure
was carefully considered
that year.

For instance, the post office
was painted red with the blood
of the unemployed on Father's Day.

Facts about

Waves

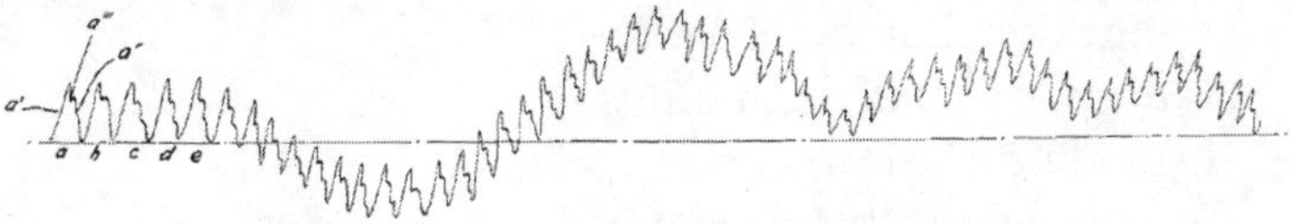

a – the duration of a wave
is the measure of time
between arriving at insight
and having the next wave
crash into your newly
opened eyes.

a^{I} – the height of a wave
enables a relational gauge
that measures Virginia Woolf's 1931
achievement against all other
attempts at understanding
collective observation.

a^{II} – the downfall of a wave
is the realization that it is,
in fact, no longer 1931 and
the gauge may be broken.

a^{III} – the hesitation of a wave's
downfall measures the momentary,
fleeting relief of not needing
comparison.

b – the repeatability of a wave
is a measure that gives meaning
to the fact of a wave.

c – the dreadfulness of a wave
is the measure of duration
extending a little too far
into the attendant insinuations
that it may never come again.

d – the pleasure of a wave
is a measure of comfortability
with variations and
evidential repeatability.

e – the courage of a wave
is measured by the overall
disturbances that propagate
energy through a medium.

After that,
who even knows
what's going on?

Facts about

Xanthippe
(For Sue and Sina)

The facts about Xanthippe
are scant: her name,
her marriage.

Her husband's words
are only reported by others,
so, really, we can't
be sure of much.

Plato's *Phaedo*
has an aside
—*you know her*—
that opens a door
to a familiarity
that could damn,
but otherwise she's depicted
as a mother and a wife
at the edge of mourning.

Xenophon's *Symposium*
gets more quickly to scorn.
Alluding, perhaps, to the roots of her name,
she is likened to a wild horse,
the most challenging to ride
to give skill to the rider.

All else has come after. References rest
on making her the ill-tempered wife. Shrew.

Shakespeare did it.
Chaucer before him.
Henry Fielding. Poe.

Another one of misogyny's idols?

Beatrice the Unrequited
Yoko the Interloper
Godiva the Temptress
Penelope the Chaste
(something else
to her suitors,
I'm sure)
Xanthippe the Nag

Joyce, a smidge more generous:
What useful discovery
did Socrates learn from Xanthippe?
Dialectic, Stephen answered,
and from his mother
how to bring thoughts
into the world.

The hard facts
are thin on the page.
Quotations and citations, sure.
Conjecture, certainly. But facts?

I'd like to imagine Xanthippe
not endlessly obliged to others,
not having to prove them
right or wrong.

I'd also like to imagine
S. singing a rendition of
"Always on My Mind" for Xanthippe
at karaoke.

What if the anniversary
of that day in Montreal
circled around again and
they asked each other:
Do you remember
where you were?

Remind me,
what time of the day
were you born?
Let's do our charts.
Let's try new cosmologies.

Each woman I've mentioned
has had an asteroid named after her
(that's something).

Unsurprisingly,
most asteroids are named
after men (that's something else).

These women
endure orbit
in the company
of their assailants
and detractors, but the
choreography of witness is clear:

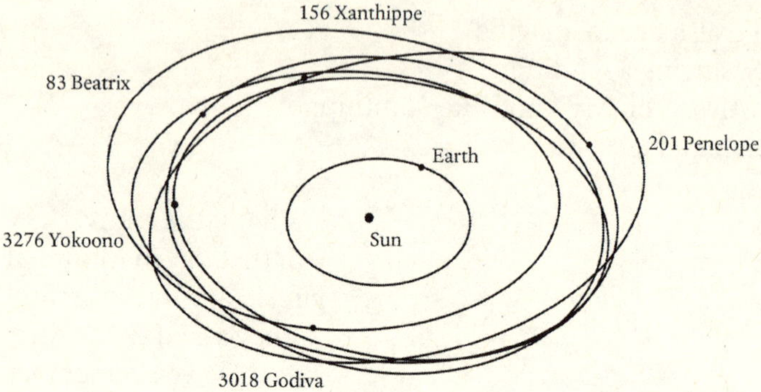

They were there, circling the sun.
They've persistently been there
and they knew: *M.L. was no young man.*

He was as old
as all the sexist,
misogynist proverbs,
as old as all the Church fathers
who doubted women had a soul.
He was as old as all the legislators
who ever forbade women the university,
the right to vote, access to the public sphere.
M.L. was as old as Man and his contempt for woman.
– Nicole Brossard,
"The Killer Was No
Young Man"

156 Xanthippe
was 326,572,152 kilometers
from Montreal on December 6, 1989.

201 Penelope
was 244,592,519 kilometers
from Montreal on December 6, 1989.

83 Beatrix
was 336,744,807 kilometers
from Montreal on December 6, 1989.

3018 Godiva
was 433,983,423 kilometers
from Montreal on December 6, 1989.

327695 Yokoono
was 395,387,172 kilometers
from Montreal on December 6, 1989.

They were there, circling the sun.
They've persistently been there.

Let's not pretend
we don't know.

Facts about Y-Axis Breaks

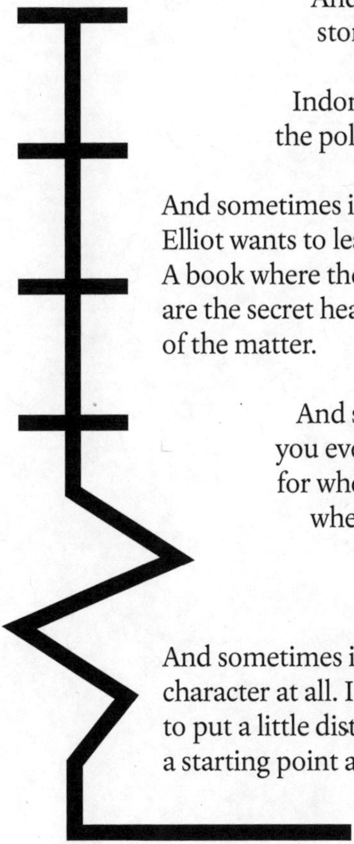

And sometimes Olie starts telling
stories in the middle. We'll never
find out how he got to that
Indonesian island, but we do know
the police escort treated him royally.

And sometimes it's the middle
Elliot wants to leave out.
A book where the endpapers
are the secret heart
of the matter.

And sometimes I don't want to tell
you everything. It's good to save bits
for when feeling whole is important,
when a good fact is just the thing.

And sometimes it's not about
character at all. It's quite helpful
to put a little distance between
a starting point and imagined heights.

Facts about the

Zodiac

It turns out the zodiac
isn't the best way
to measure space.

Ecliptic measurements figure
a celestial coordinate system:
Just like its earthly cousin,
it pits latitude against longitude
and declares space mapped.

But a spat erupted
where things were supposed
to be equal.

One drank too much.
The other's eyes wandered.
Et tu, llongitūdō?

The celebrations
got carried away.

They've been
drifting ever since.

Fact
or no fact
in the stars,
material is made
and we circle around,
look skyward,
or flip through pages
to catch a glimpse
of a better earth.

Perhaps it's not so odd
to look for some clarity in print.

Lakes of ink
have been dedicated to
this unearthly view.

The periodical press alone
must be approaching
ink proportions
close to Shakespeare,
King James,
and the DSM-5.

Though somewhat abandoned
as the standard record-keeping
scheme, sky creatures,
much like poetry,
can provide unusual truth
by virtue of being organized
outside the rules
of factual expectancy.

While outmoded,
don't dismiss the zodiac just yet,
ye realists of the sky. A sea-goat
is still a remarkable thing
to summon, though
a strange god indeed.

Sky sculptures make lousy yardsticks,
but inadequate sticks make great kindling.

NOTES

FACTS ABOUT ALLOTHEISM

For a unique history of anagrams, see: Wheatley, Henry Benjamin. *Of anagrams: a monograph treating of their history from the earliest ages to the present time, with an introduction, containing numerous specimens of macaronic poetry, punning mottoes, rhopalic, shaped, equivocal, Lyon, and echo verses, alliteration, acrostics, lipograms, chronograms, logograms, palindromes, bouts rimes*. 1862. Kessinger, 2006.

For information on Holmes's theories of continental drift, see: Holmes, Arthur. *Principles of Physical Geology*. T. Nelson and Sons, 1948.

Lithos is used in the California state parks logo, but is certainly not allowed to be used for brochures or park signs: "Fonts and colors for California State Parks branding are designed to help convey the warm, down-to-earth, adventurous and approachable nature of the parks themselves." *California State Parks Brand Standards Handbook.* State of California, 2007.

FACTS ABOUT BRAZIL NUTS

These nutters don't think the Brazil rises to the top: Metzger, Matthew J., Remy, Brenda, and Glasser, Benjamin J. "All the Brazil Nuts Are Not on Top: Vibration Induced Granular Size Segregation of Binary, Ternary and Multi-sized Mixtures." *Powder Technology* 205.1, 2011: 42–51.

Thomson, Christine, Alexandra Chisholm, Sarah McLachlan, and Jennifer Campbell. "Brazil Nuts: An Effective Way to Improve Selenium Status." *The American Journal of Clinical Nutrition* 87.2, 2008.

"Brazil Nuts." *Radioactive Consumer Products*, 20 Jan 2009.

FACTS ABOUT CONTINENTAL DRIFT

Dunham, K. C. "Arthur Holmes. 1890–1965." *Biographical Memoirs of Fellows of the Royal Society.* Vol. 12, 1966: 291–310.

For a ground-shaking read, see Henry R. Frankel, *The Continental Drift Controversy* (4 volumes). Cambridge University Press; 2012.

FACTS ABOUT DAYS (BAD)

Facts about seconds gleaned from the website of the Bureau International des Poids et Mesures: www.bipm.org

J.K. Rowling wrote a series of novels based around the shenanigans of a young lad named Harry James Potter and his friends. If you've not read them, or not at least seen the movies, you're missing out on some *pretty interesting* dreams. If you've not even heard of the boy, you might examine your life a little closer.

FACTS ABOUT FACTS

Anderson, Laurie, with William S. Burroughs. "Sharkey's Night." *Mister Heartbreak*. Warner Brothers, 1984.

My dictionary: *The Oxford Universal Dictionary*. Oxford: Oxford UP, 1955.

FACTS ABOUT GARDENING

For a discussion of touching plants, which references Charlie's talking habits, see: Day, Sonia. "Prince Charles talks to his plants—I caress mine." *The Star*. 22 May 2010.

FACTS ABOUT AN HERBARIUM

Dickinson, Emily, 1830–1886. *Herbarium*, circa 1839–1846. 1 volume (66 pages) in green cloth case; 37 cm. MS Am 1118.11, Houghton Library.

"system of aesthetics / far superior to mine." is from Dickenson's "Flowers—Well—if anybody" First published in *Drum Beat*, Brooklyn. 2 March 1864.

FACTS ABOUT INVISIBLE INK

How to be a Spy: The World War II SOE Training Manual. Toronto: The Dundurn Group, 2004: 234–247.

Reader, please insert citation for passage printed in invisible ink once you've figured out how to reveal the stanza (I've left enough space, I think):

FACTS ABOUT JUGGLING

Defoe, Daniel. *A system of magick; or, a history of the black art: Being an historical account of mankind's most early dealing with the Devil; and how the acquaintance on both sides first begun.* London: printed and sold by Andrew Millar, 1728.

For a history of the International Jugglers' Association, see: www.juggle.org/history

For a broad history of juggling, see: Truzzi, Marcello, with Massimiliano Truzzi. "Notes Toward a History of Juggling." *Bandwagon* 18.2, March–April 1974.

FACTS ABOUT LOVE

The existence of "luck" has been a subject of long debate... into which I dare not wade for fear of my love being jinxed.

FACTS ABOUT MANGOES

There is no extent evidence that Thomas Pynchon, Jane Austen, or Jarvis Cocker, *didn't* mention mangoes in early—now misplaced—drafts of their work or that an unused—now lost—"take" recorded for *Field of Dreams* did not have Kevin Costner mention mangoes. As for me, you be the judge.

Oliver, Mary. "The Mango." *Poetry* (March 1986): 329.

Grant, Eddy. "Drop, Baby, Drop." *Killer on the Rampage.* Portrait, 1982.

Salman Rushdie gave this advice while receiving a lifetime achievement award from the Asian American Writers Workshop at Tribeca in New York in 2013.

FACTS ABOUT NICOLAS SANSON

The map in question is: Sanson, Nicolas (the elder). "Guiane divisee en Guiane, et Caribane." *L'Amérique en plusieurs cartes nouvelles et exactes*. Np: Paris, 1657.

For more information on Nic, see: Chisholm, Hugh, ed. "Sanson, Nicolas." *Encyclopædia Britannica*. 24 (11th ed.). Cambridge University Press: 183.

FACTS ABOUT OLATHE SLIM

For more on Earl Browder, see the Earl Browder Papers at Syracuse University.

For more on marbled endpapers from the 1840s, see: Wolfe, Richard J. *Marbled Paper: Its History, Techniques and Patterns.* University of Pennsylvania Press, 1991.

FACTS ABOUT QUAKING ASPEN

This was written after a studio visit with Graeme Patterson and Rita McKeough as they were preparing for *Murmurations*, a collaborative exhibition at the Owens Art Gallery in Sackville, New Brunswick. For more, see: Wunker, Erin, et al. *Murmurations: New Work by Graeme Patterson and Rita McKeough.* Owens Art Gallery, Mount Allison University, 2017. This is humbly dedicated to Graeme and Rita.

"Quaking Aspen." National Parks Service, U.S. Department of the Interior.

FACTS ABOUT REMEMORATION AND RAIN DOGS

Quotations come from the opening lines of: Derrida, Jacques, et al. "The Purveyor of Truth." *Yale French Studies*, 52 (1975): 31–113.

"R" words were generously generated by the inimitable Jerry Marshall Ropson via text message, i.e., electronic telegram.

FACTS ABOUT SWEARING (A PRAYER FOR MY DAUGHTER)

"hearts are not had as a gift / but hearts are earned" is from W.B. Yeats's "A Prayer for my Daughter." See: Yeats, *W. B. Collected Poems. Definitive Ed., with the Authors Final Revisions.* Macmillan, 1956.

"as it were, / learning this art ever anew / from the lips of the Divine Master himself" is from Pope John Paul II's text for the 42nd "World Day of Prayer."

For a history of "Oh Susanna," see: Bernstein, Jonathan. "OH! SUSANNA." *Oxford American: A magazine of the South.* 20 August 2012.

Simone, Nina. "Mississippi Goddamn." *Nina Simone in Concert*. Philips, 1964.

FACTS ABOUT TELEGRAMS AND TEXT MESSAGES

For more information on Neil Papworth and his text message, see: www.neilpapworth.com

For information on the last telegram sent by Western Union, see: Freierman, Shelly. "Telegram Falls Silent Stop Era Ends Stop." *The New York Times*, 6 Feb 2006.

"The razor-toothed piranhas of the genera Serrasalmus and Pygocentrus are the most ferocious freshwater fish in the world. In reality they seldom attack a human." is the official prompt for the measurement of texting speed. For current news on the record, see: Janela, Mike. "Fastest Touch-Screen Text Message Record Officially Broken with Fleksy Keyboard." *Guinness World Records*, 19 May 2014.

FACTS ABOUT UNTRUTHS

For up-to-date numbers, see The Fact Checker's ongoing database of the false or misleading claims made by President Trump since assuming office:
www.washingtonpost.com.

For more information on the history of lie detectors and Leonarde Keeler, see: Alder, Ken. *The Lie Detectors: The History of an American Obsession*. Univ. of Nebraska Press, 2009.

FACTS ABOUT VANCOUVER, 1938

"No Asiatic person shall be employed in or upon any part of the undertaking or other works" is a well-known provision attached to the building of the construction of the Lions' Gate Bridge by the Guinness family and others. For more information on the bridge, see: Fleming, Andrew. "Archives: Lions Gate Bridge Opens to Traffic." *Vancouver Courier*, 13 November 2014, and "Assembling the Lions Gate Bridge." *Skyrise Vancouver News*.

For information on the 1938 Sitdown Strike or Bloody Sunday, see: Marsh, James. "Bloody Sunday." *The Canadian Encyclopedia*. Toronto: Historica Canada, 2012.

FACTS ABOUT WAVES

Figure of waves from Lenoarde Keeler's 1931 Patent (US1788434A) for his Apparatus for Recording Arterial Blood Pressure.

FACTS ABOUT XANTHIPPE

This was written after reading Sina Queyras's *Lemon Hound* interview with Sue Goyette, "Women, Epic, Live Wires: In Conversation with Sue Goyette," in December 2017, and is humbly dedicated to Sina and Sue.

Asteroid positions were determined using NASA's Jet Propulsion Laboratory Small-Body Database: *https://ssd.jpl.nasa.gov/sbdb.cgi*.

James Joyce quotation is from *Ulysses*.

Ideally, Socrates would sing the Willie Nelson version of "Always on My Mind," which Willie recorded in 1982, but I could also imagine a particularly rowdy night when it would be totally appropriate to sing the Pet Shop Boys' version, which they recorded in 1987 and was the UK Christmas single that year. Love and respect might happen in country crooning or synthpop styling. I'm OK with that. I can only hope Xanthippe would be OK with either version too.

Brossard, Nicole. "The Killer Was No Young Man." *La Presse* 21 December 1989.

FACTS ABOUT THE ZODIAC

DSM-5: *Diagnostic and Statistical Manual of Mental Disorders* (5th Ed). American Psychiatric Association, 2013.

ACKNOWLEDGEMENTS

Thanks to those friends who have listened, talked, read, nourished, and sustained during the writing and revision of this book, including, but not limited to: Nolan Natasha, Jerry Ropson, Graeme Patterson, Bucky Buckler and Robin Walker, Michael McCormack, Paul Henderson, Amy Siegel, Steve Lambke, Lou Sheppard, Geordie Miller, Marc Fortin, Hannah McGregor, Carrie Dawson, and Katherine Victoria Taylor and Joe Landry at the Dawson Print Shop.

A previous version of "Facts about Xanthippe" appeared in *Lemon Hound*.

A previous version of "Facts about Quaking Aspen" appeared in *Visual Arts News*.

Sachiko Murakami, Stephen Collis, and Kate Siklosi have generously favoured the book with their words. I thank them for their careful reading, their time, and for their own vital work.

The crew at Invisible Publishing deserve many thanks: Leigh Nash for her patience, Andrew Faulkner for his enthusiasm and acute editorial eye, and Megan Fildes for her design.

For everything, E & e.

INVISIBLE PUBLISHING produces fine Canadian literature for those who enjoy such things. As a not-for-profit publisher, our work includes building communities that sustain and encourage engaging, literary, and current writing.

Invisible Publishing has been in operation for over a decade. We released our first fiction titles in the spring of 2007, and our catalogue has come to include works of graphic fiction and non-fiction, pop culture biographies, experimental poetry, and prose.

We are committed to publishing diverse voices and experiences. In acknowledging historical and systemic barriers, and the limits of our existing catalogue, we strongly encourage LGBTQ2SIA+, Indigenous, and writers of colour to submit their work.

Invisible Publishing is also home to the Bibliophonic series of music books and the Throwback series of CanLit reissues.

If you'd like to know more, please get in touch:
info@invisiblepublishing.com